JESUS'
HIGH VIEW
OF
SCRIPTURE

TOM PENNINGTON

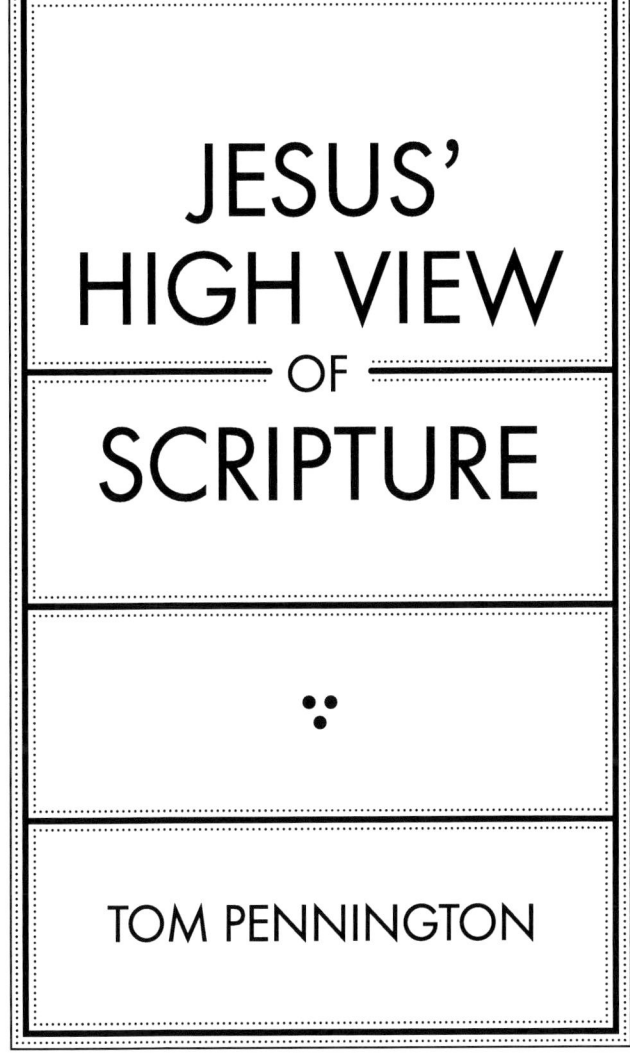

JESUS' HIGH VIEW
OF
SCRIPTURE

TOM PENNINGTON

THE WORD UNLEASHED
A Ministry of Countryside Bible Church
Southlake, TX

Jesus' High View of Scripture
by Tom Pennington

Unless otherwise indicated, all Scripture quotations are
taken from the New American Standard Bible ®, © 1960, 1962,
1963, 1968, 1971, 1972, 1973, 1975, 1977, 1995 by the Lock-
man Foundation. Used by permission. (www.Lockman.org)

Design by MOOSE77.com

Jesus' High View of Scripture
© 2021 by Tom Pennington
Published by © The Word Unleashed
www.thewordunleashed.org
PO Box 96077, Southlake, TX 76092

The Word Unleashed is a ministry of
Countryside Bible Church in Southlake, TX.
www.countrysidebible.org
ISBN - 978-0-578-91167-0

Print in the United States of America

To the elders of Countryside Bible Church,
whose love for the Scripture have made serving
with them one of my life's greatest joys

CONTENTS

∴

"Do not think that I came to abolish the Law or the Prophets; I did not come to abolish but to fulfill. For truly I say to you, until heaven and earth pass away, not the smallest letter or stroke shall pass from the Law until all is accomplished. Whoever then annuls one of the least of these commandments, and teaches others to do the same, shall be called least in the kingdom of heaven; but whoever keeps and teaches them, he shall be called great in the kingdom of heaven.

"For I say to you that unless your righteousness surpasses that of the scribes and Pharisees, you will not enter the kingdom of heaven."

MATTHEW 5:17–20

⁘

INTRODUCTION

⁘

ABOUT 50 miles north of the city of Los Angeles is a monument that marks one of the worst disasters in California history. The St. Francis Dam was 600 feet long and 185 feet high and was completed on March 1, 1926. Just two years later on March 12, 1928, the dam failed. A 180-foot-high wall of water came crashing down San Francisquito Canyon. By the time the floodwaters reached the Pacific Ocean five and a half hours later, 470 people were dead. In terms of lives lost, it was the second-worst disaster in California history, second only to the great San Francisco earthquake and fire of 1906.

William Mulholland, the famous engineer, had designed the dam, and when he learned of the disaster, he was devastated. In fact, he never recovered. As investigators searched for a cause, they learned that the dam itself was structurally sound. But it was doomed from the beginning, because it was built on a bad foundation. At the time there was no way Mulholland could have known that the ground on which the dam was built was itself fatally flawed and its collapse was inevitable.

The same problem manifests itself in religion and philosophy. The superstructure may appear reasonably sound, but if the foundational authority is flawed, the entire belief system is at risk of complete collapse. Every religion or philosophy has an ultimate, foundational authority. It is the bedrock foundation on which it stands—the person, writings, or ideas to which its adherents ultimately appeal as their final authority. There are many different sources of such authority but most, like Mulholland's dam, are tragically flawed.

Some rely on sacred writings. Buddhism rests on the written sayings of Buddha, Islam on Mohammed and the Koran, and Mormonism on the writings of Joseph Smith. Others place their confidence in man himself. In the philosophy of naturalism, the authority is the cosmos as interpreted by humanistic scientists. Empiricism finds its ultimate authority in the human senses and rationalism in human reason.

The world is increasingly filled with those who create their own unique religion or philosophy. We have designer clothes, designer dogs, and now designer faiths. Such people look at the available ideas, philosophies, and religions as a buffet line from which they can select what appeals to them. "I'll have a little Christianity. I think Jesus was a wonderful teacher and the Bible contains some great and enlightening thoughts. And I like the experientialism of Eastern Mysticism, so put some of that on my plate as well. I like that post-modernism says truth and ethics are relative, so I'll take some of that too." This is how many approach what they believe. It's Mr. Potato Head faith—choose the parts you like and then put them where you want them. Such people truly become their own ultimate authority.

For believers, of course, our ultimate source of authority is the Bible. But why do we believe the Bible? There are several legitimate answers to that question, but one primary reason is the testimony of Jesus Christ our Lord. We believe the Old Testament because He affirmed it to be the very words of the living God. We believe the New Testament because He pre-authenticated it by choosing the men who would either write it or under whose auspices it would be written.

The first main point of Jesus' most famous sermon, the Sermon on the Mount, is that the only legitimate source of authority is God's written Word. And He demands that His disciples believe exactly *as* He does about the Bible—*because* He does.

The Sermon on the Mount consists of three basic parts: an introduction, the body of the sermon, and a conclusion.[1] In the introduction Jesus identifies the citizens of His spiritual kingdom by describing their character in the qualities we know as the beatitudes (5:3-12). Because His followers consistently demonstrate those qualities, their influence is like salt in the midst of decay and light in the midst of darkness (5:13-16).

The heart of the sermon describes the righteousness of the kingdom (Matt. 5:17—7:12). Jesus teaches us how we should live in the spiritual kingdom over which He rules.

The first and primary expression of kingdom righteousness is having a right relationship to the Scripture (5:17-48). Jesus explains what our relationship to Scripture should be (5:17-20) and then provides six examples that confronted and corrected rabbinic misunderstandings (5:21-47).

The core of the sermon begins and ends with this same theme. It begins, "Do not think that I came to abolish the Law or the Prophets; I did not come to abolish but to fulfill" (5:17). Jesus ends the body of the sermon by saying, "In everything, therefore, treat people the same way you want them to treat you, for this is the Law and the Prophets" (7:12). He intentionally bracketed the heart of His sermon with references to the Law and the Prophets, because the Sermon on the Mount is His exegesis of how to understand and practice the Scripture. He clearly stated the proposition of His message in Matthew 5:17-20:

> *Do not think that I came to abolish the Law or the Prophets; I did not come to abolish but to fulfill. For truly I say to you, until heaven and earth pass away, not the smallest letter or stroke shall pass from the Law until all is accomplished. Whoever then annuls one of the least of these commandments, and teaches others to do the same, shall be called least in the kingdom of heaven; but whoever keeps and teaches them, he shall be called great in the kingdom of heaven. For I say to you that unless your righteousness surpasses that of the scribes and Pharisees, you will not enter the kingdom of heaven.*

Jesus was concerned that His disciples not misunderstand their relationship to Scripture, so He began,

"Do not think..." (17). He wanted to ensure we avoid two great dangers. One danger is to think that once you become a follower of Jesus the Old Testament no longer matters, that you are free to abandon it and listen only to Him. The other danger is to copy the external legalism of the scribes and Pharisees and miss the whole point of the Old Testament. Jesus addressed both dangers.

True subjects of Jesus' spiritual kingdom can always be recognized by how they respond to the Scripture, by how they think about and treat the Word of God. In these verses, Jesus identifies *three responses* to Scripture that should characterize every genuine believer: We must 1) understand Jesus' own relationship to Scripture (17), 2) embrace His view of Scripture (18), and 3) accept His diagnosis using the Scripture (19-20). We will briefly consider the first and third responses but focus primarily on Jesus' view of Scripture and the resulting imperative that all who follow Him must embrace the same view.

CHAPTER ONE

UNDERSTAND JESUS' OWN RELATIONSHIP TO SCRIPTURE

"Do not think that I came to abolish the Law or the Prophets;
I did not come to abolish but to fulfill."

MATTHEW 5:17

⁚

A S JESUS began His ministry, there were understandable questions about His relationship to God's previous revelation. Wanting to remove any confusion, He began, "Do not think that I came to abolish the Law or the Prophets; I did not come to abolish but to fulfill" (17). He wanted His disciples to understand His own relationship to the Hebrew Scripture.

In the first century, there was a definitive list of books that were accepted as divinely inspired. Jesus called them "the Law and the Prophets." The books Jesus referred to, the books that constituted the Jewish canon of the first century, contained exactly the same content as our Old Testament today, although the numeration was different.

Instead of 39 books as in our OT, the Jewish canon included 22 books or 24 books, depending on how various books were combined. For example, each of the two books of Samuel, Kings, and Chronicles were typically combined into single books, and at times Kings and Chronicles were placed together. Ezra and Nehemiah were also combined. And the twelve minor prophets were always considered as one book. So, the OT canon of the first century had a different number of books than our OT, but exactly the same content.

The 39 books identified as the Old Testament in our Bibles—and only those books[1]—were unequivocally held in Jesus' time to be the Word of God. That the OT canon was completely settled by the time of Jesus Christ is the common view of Jewish scholarship. Jewish tradition says Ezra and Malachi were part of the Great Synagogue that collected, preserved, and confirmed the final canon of the OT, 400 years before Jesus. Here, Jesus confirmed that with His own testimony. Specifically, He made two assertions about how His followers are to understand His relationship to the Scripture.

First, He denied that He came to abolish the Hebrew Scripture. He insisted we reject the idea that He had come to demolish or to tear down by His teaching the content or authority of the Old Testament Scripture.

It is possible Jesus' enemies leveled this charge against Him during His lifetime. Although there is no record that His enemies directly accused Him of wanting to abolish the OT, this accusation was later leveled against His disciples. During the earliest days of the church, Jewish antagonists in Jerusalem

Secretly induced men to say, 'We have heard Stephen speak blasphemous words against Moses.'... They put forward false witnesses who said, 'This man incessantly speaks against this holy place and the Law; for we have heard him say that this Nazarene, Jesus, will destroy this place and alter the customs which Moses handed down to us' (Acts 6:11, 13).

The same accusation was made against Paul. "While Gallio was proconsul of Achaia, the Jews with one accord rose up against Paul and brought him before the judgment seat, saying, 'This man persuades men to worship God contrary to the Law'" (Acts 18:12-13). Jesus often violated His enemies' tradition, their misguided interpretation of the Old Testament. Of course, the flashpoint was the Sabbath. When Jesus refused to follow their traditions, they believed He was violating the Old Testament, because they believed their interpretations were on par with Scripture itself. But Jesus never violated God's law, only their mistaken interpretation.

It is possible that even Jesus' disciples were confused about His relationship to the Old Testament. So, He said, "Do not think that I came to abolish the Old Testament Scripture." The Greek word *abolish* means "to demolish or to tear down a structure." It is even used of destroying the temple (Matt. 24:2). When this word refers to an authoritative text, it means to declare it no longer valid or binding. Jesus did not teach that His disciples no longer needed to respect or obey the Hebrew Scripture.

Secondly, He insisted He had come to *fulfill* the Old Testament. To *fulfill* is an expression itself full of meaning. He fulfilled the Old Testament 1) by perfectly revealing its meaning in His teaching (Matt. 5:21-22, 27-28, 31-32, 33-34, 38-39, 43-44), 2) by perfectly obeying it in His life (Matt. 3:15; John 8:46; 15:10; Gal. 4:4-5), and 3) by bringing its message to complete fruition in His own life and ministry—He embodied the OT ideas, ceremonies, and pictures in His own person (Luke 24:27, 44-48; John 5:39; Col. 2:16-17; Heb. 10:1-12). It is crucial that Jesus' followers understand His own relationship to Scripture—that He explained it in His teaching, obeyed it in His life, and embodied it in His person.

The second response that all who belong to Jesus' kingdom must have toward the Scripture is the central focus of this book.

CHAPTER TWO

EMBRACE JESUS' VIEW OF SCRIPTURE

"For truly I say to you, until heaven and earth pass away,
not the smallest letter or stroke shall pass from the Law
until all is accomplished."

MATTHEW 5:18

⋮

"FOR truly I say to you" is a familiar way our Lord introduced His most strategic statements. The word for means that verse 18 provides the reason Jesus did not come to abolish the Old Testament but to fulfill it: His high view of Scripture. The Greek word for *truly* is *amen*—a Hebrew word transliterated into Greek and then into English. It can be translated as *this is true* or *let it be true*. The entire expression calls for careful attention because what Jesus is about to say is firm, reliable, and certain.

This was Jesus' unique way to add veritas, weight, and solemnity. In Matthew's gospel alone, He used this expression 31 times. Here, He used it to underscore His view of Scripture. He tells us what He believed about the Old Testament, and what we should therefore believe as well. What follows is one of the most powerful, compelling statements Jesus ever made: "For truly I say to you, until heaven and earth pass away, not the smallest letter or stroke shall pass from the Law until all is accomplished" (18). That is not a statement to read past quickly. It is a profound, life-changing statement from the mouth of our Lord about the nature of Scripture.

Instead of repeating the expression the *Law or the Prophets* (17), He shortened it to the Law (18) but still meant the entire Old Testament. The New Testament often uses the word *Law* of the entire Old Testament. For example, John 10:34, 12:34, and 15:25 all quote the book of Psalms but refer to it as the *Law*. In 1 Corinthians 14:21 Paul quotes Isaiah and says that it was written in *the Law*. In Romans 3:19, he strings together a series of verses from both the Psalms and the Prophets and says they were written in *the Law*. Here in Matthew 5:18, Jesus is also referring to the entire Old Testament.

In this powerful statement, Jesus affirmed in the strongest possible terms His unwavering confidence in several unchanging attributes of Scripture!

∵

SCRIPTURE'S ETERNAL AUTHORITY

∵

The first attribute Jesus affirms is its *eternal authority*. "Truly I say to you, until heaven and earth pass away..." (18). There are two possible meanings of that expression.

Jesus may have been referring to the coming day when the present heavens and earth, the universe as we know it, will be completely destroyed. Second Peter 3:10 describes that day: "The day of the Lord will come like a thief, in which the heavens will pass away with a roar and the elements will be destroyed with intense heat, and the earth and its works will be burned up." Jesus may have been making the point that God's Word will endure as long as this present universe stands—until it's completely destroyed.

More likely, however, He used these words in a common proverbial way that simply means never. That is how He used this same expression in a similar context in Luke 16:17: "It is easier for heaven and earth to pass away than for one stroke of a letter of the Law to fail." Jesus contrasted the likelihood of heaven and earth being destroyed with the likelihood of any part of the Law being destroyed or annulled. His point is that it is far easier for the universe to go out of existence entirely than for the smallest stroke of a letter of God's Word to fail. His Word is more enduring than the universe itself. According to Jesus, it will never fail. It will survive even if everything else is completely destroyed. It is permanent. Unchanging. Eternal.

In Psalm 119:89 the Psalmist writes, "Forever, O Lord, Your word is settled in heaven." Literally, "Your word stands firm in heaven." It is not tied to this planet and what happens here but stands firm in heaven itself—not the heavens in which the stars and galaxies move, but the heaven which God Himself occupies. Psalm 119:152 says,

"Of old I have known from Your testimonies that You have founded them forever." Isaiah 40:8 adds, "The grass withers, the flower fades, but the word of our God stands forever." Things on this planet constantly change, and the planet itself will one day disappear. But the Word of God is the one stable, permanent, enduring reality.

Jesus said the same thing about His own words. In the Olivet discourse, as He described events that will unfold in the future, He said, "Heaven and earth will pass away, but My words will not pass away" (Matt. 24:35). Everything we see will go out of existence. God will destroy it all. But what Jesus said will never go out of existence!

The rest of the New Testament has the same eternal authority. Paul refers to Luke's gospel as Scripture (1 Tim. 5:18) and Peter identifies Paul's letters as Scripture (2 Pet. 3:15-16). Since the New Testament is also Scripture, Paul demanded that every church acknowledge that he and the other apostles wrote the commands of Christ (1 Cor. 14:37) and that churches obey the apostles' commands, including their written words (1 Cor. 11:2; 2 Th. 2:5). All who refuse to obey the apostles' words are to be put out of the church (2 Th. 3:6, 14). The words of the apostles have the same permanent authority as the Old Testament and Jesus' own words, because ultimately, they came from Christ Himself. Jesus authenticated the Old Testament Scripture. And He pre-authenticated the New Testament by choosing the men who would write under His authority, giving His commands through His Spirit. His words, like the words of the Old Testament, will never pass away.

There are two key implications of Scripture's eternal authority. First, it must be the ultimate authority for all who follow Jesus. If God has spoken and what He says has permanent authority, we should believe it and it should direct how we live. And, secondly, if Scripture has eternal authority, it is eternally relevant. After the resurrection, Jesus gave the Great Commission to the 500 disciples gathered on a mountain in Galilee (Matt. 28:18-20). He told them to go to all the nations. After they had made disciples and baptized them, they were to teach them all that He had commanded. And that mission was to continue "even to the end of the age." In every time and place what Jesus taught is eternally authoritative and therefore relevant. He believed and taught Scripture's eternal authority.

∵

SCRIPTURE'S VERBAL INSPIRATION

∵

"Not the smallest letter or stroke shall pass from the Law" (18). Jesus also believed Scripture's *verbal inspiration*. Theologians use those two words to explain what the Scripture teaches about itself and what our Lord teaches in this verse. The English word inspiration comes from the Latin Vulgate translation of 2 Timothy 3:16, where Jerome mistakenly used the Latin word *inspirata*, which means "to breathe into." But the Greek word translated *inspired* is *theopneustas*, which literally means "God-breathed." All Scripture is *breathed out by God* in the sense that He spoke it. Scripture is the product of God's breath, just as the words we speak are the product of our breath. B. B. Warfield wrote, "The Greek term has...nothing to say of *inspiring* or of *inspiration*.... What it says of Scripture is, not that it is 'breathed into by God'...but that it is breathed out by God, 'God-breathed,' the product of the creative breath of God."[1] He adds, "To hear the Scripture is to hear God speak."[2] That is inspiration. The word *verbal* means that God is the source of not only the thoughts of Scripture, but also the very words. Through His Spirit, God breathed out every single word in the original autographs.

This is what the church has believed and taught for 2,000 years. Origen, one of the early church fathers, wrote, "Every reader [of Scripture] reverentially understands that he is dealing with divine and non-human words inserted in the sacred books."[3] He wasn't denying there were human authors—he believed and taught that. Rather, he was affirming that the ultimate source of the words was not the human author but God Himself. Another of the early church fathers, Hippolytus, described this using an image common among the church fathers:

> *Just as it is with musical instruments, so they always had the Word, like the pick, in union with them, and when moved by him, the prophets announced what God willed. For they did not speak of their own power (let there be no mistake as to that), neither did they declare what pleased themselves.* [4]

The writers of Scripture were like a musical instrument. And the word was a pick and the Holy Spirit the player, strumming out the tune He wanted. The instrument was involved, of course. But the One who was playing produced the music He wanted—down to the very words.

Some argue that verbal inspiration was a fabrication of the early church or the Reformers. But according to this text it was exactly what Jesus Himself believed. And His confidence in Scripture was reflected in His teaching. There were times when He based His entire argument on a single word in the Hebrew text. In Mark 12, He asked the religious leaders if the Messiah would be the son of David. They vacillated but eventually answered that Messiah would be David's son. Jesus responded by asking them why David had said, "The Lord says to my Lord" (Mark 12:36; cf. Ps. 110:1). Jesus based His argument on the Hebrew pronoun *my*. The Messiah has to be greater than David and not just his physical descendant because David calls Him "*my* Lord." Jesus chose one word—a pronoun—from the Hebrew Old Testament to argue for the deity of the Messiah.

But Jesus went even further than insisting the individual words of Scripture are inspired. He said, "Not the smallest letter or stroke shall pass from the Law" (18). Literally, the Greek text reads, "One *iota* or one little horn, no not at all, shall pass away." The *iota* is the smallest Greek letter, that Jesus used here to refer to the smallest Hebrew letter, *yod*. It is the equivalent of our English letter *y* and looks like an English apostrophe.

Linguists tell us there are more than 66,000 *yods* in the Old Testament. So how important can one apostrophe-sized letter be? How much would it undermine God's truth if one of 66,000 was omitted? Jesus guaranteed that not one will pass away!

But Jesus went still further. Next, He used a Greek word that points to a single *stroke* of a Hebrew letter. Literally, it is "a horn" or anything that projects like a horn, such as the part of a letter. It refers to a pen stroke that distinguishes one letter from another. In English, such a stroke is the only difference between a capital O and Q. The same is true in Hebrew. The Hebrew letters B (b), *bet*, and K (k), *kaf*, are almost identical, except for a little protrusion in the lower right-hand corner. The Hebrew letters D (d), *dalet*, and R (r), *resh* are also only distinguished by a similar pen stroke. There are countless such pen strokes in the Old Testament. Jesus said that not one will lose its force or become invalid. Not one!

Jesus was making the remarkable claim that the Old Testament Scripture is breathed out by God, not only in its individual words and letters, but even the smallest strokes that distinguish one letter from another! R. Laird Harris, in *The Inspiration and Canonicity of Scripture*, writes, "Jesus declared that the Scriptures were letter perfect."[5]

That is what Jesus believed and taught about the Old and New Testaments. And it is what He expects His followers to believe as well, on the basis of His authority.

∵

SCRIPTURE'S PLENARY INSPIRATION

∵

A third attribute of Scripture Jesus affirms is *plenary inspiration*. The theological term *plenary* simply means *all*. All Scripture is breathed out by God. In verse 18, He said not one of the smallest letters or a single stroke will pass away from the Law until all is accomplished. But in verse 17, Jesus referred to the entire Old Testament. Not only is each individual stroke, letter, and word breathed out by God, but all of it in its entirety is as well. Jesus affirmed the individual parts of the Old Testament—*every* stroke, letter, and word. But He also affirmed the whole to be the Word of God—*all* its strokes letters, and words. In Inerrancy John Wenham writes:

> *Christ held the Old Testament to be historically true, completely authoritative, and divinely inspired. To him, the God of the Old Testament was the living God, and the teaching of the Old Testament was the teaching of the living God. To him, what Scripture said, God said.*[6]

During His ministry, Jesus affirmed many historical details recorded in the Old Testament. He confirmed as historically accurate the Genesis 1 and 2 record of creation, the creation of a historical Adam and Eve, their marriage, the fall of man in the garden, the murder of Abel, and the reality of Noah and the flood. He affirmed the days of Lot and the divine destruction of Sodom and Gomorrah. He cited the giving of the law at Sinai, the Ten Commandments, and Moses lifting up the bronze serpent in the wilderness. He mentioned Jacob's giving a field to Joseph. He affirmed the Mosaic authorship of the Pentateuch, a famine in the days of Elijah, and Naaman the Syrian being cleansed of leprosy by Elisha. He treated as history the queen of Sheba meeting Solomon, Jonah surviving three days in the belly of a great fish, Jonah's message to Nineveh, the repentance of the people of Nineveh, and the stoning of Zechariah. In the gospel record, our Lord confirmed all those historical facts recorded in the Old Testament, along with many others.

If you are a disciple of Jesus Christ, you must believe what He believed about the Old Testament. You must believe that it is breathed out by God, not only its letters and strokes but *all* of it. You must believe what it teaches about the way of salvation and the way the world was created. Some who desire to synchronize the Bible with modern science argue that the theological statements of Scripture are true but the scientific and historical statements are not necessarily accurate. But if one word of Scripture is in error, none of it can be trusted, because we have no mechanism or apparatus to definitively distinguish what is true from what is not.

Augustine wrote:

The most disastrous consequences must follow upon our believing that anything false is found in the sacred books.... For if you once admit into such a high sanctuary of authority one false statement..., there will not be left a single sentence of those books which, if appearing to anyone difficult in practice or hard to believe, may not by the same fatal rule be explained away. [7]

If God did not destroy the cities of Sodom and Gomorrah with fire and brimstone as Scripture teaches, how do we know there is only one true God as it teaches elsewhere? If Jonah was not swallowed by a great fish, how can we have confidence that God will extend mercy to repentant Gentiles, which is the message of Jonah's prophecy? The historical facts and the redemptive promises rise and fall together. Our Lord had complete confidence in the *plenary* inspiration of the Scripture—all of it was breathed out by God. You and I must affirm it as well.

∵

SCRIPTURE'S COMPLETE INERRANCY

∵

Jesus not only believed in Scripture's eternal authority, its verbal inspiration, and its plenary inspiration, but also its complete inerrancy. "For truly I say to you, until heaven and earth pass away, not the smallest letter or stroke shall pass from the Law, until all is accomplished" (18). That is a statement of the truthfulness, certainty, and trustworthiness of all Scripture, down to every letter and stroke. It is what theologians call *inerrancy*.

In defining inerrancy Paul Feinberg writes, "When all the facts become known they will demonstrate that the Bible, in its original autographs and correctly interpreted, is entirely true and never false in all it affirms."[8] That includes all the doctrine of Scripture, such as Scripture's claims about itself, the way of salvation, man's nature as a sinner, the character of God, and its eschatology. Everything Scripture affirms in its doctrine is true and never false. But it also includes everything Scripture affirms in its ethics: the sinfulness of homosexuality, adultery, lust, and pride and the priorities of loving God with a whole heart and loving others as ourselves. Inerrancy affirms that Scripture is without error and speaks the entire truth in everything. That means when Scripture speaks of the social, physical, and life sciences, it is never in error, when properly interpreted.

The two arguments for biblical inerrancy are historical and biblical. The historical argument contends that throughout church history, the church has spoken with one voice on this issue. Gregg Allison in *Historical Theology* writes:

> The church has historically acknowledged that Scripture in its original manuscripts and properly interpreted is completely true and without any error in everything that it affirms, whether that has to do with doctrine, moral conduct, or matters of history, cosmology, geography, and the like. Over time, the church has expressed this conviction by applying a number of terms to the Bible,

such as truthful, inerrant, and infallible. No matter what
term it used, the church from its outset was united in its
belief that the Word of God is true and contains no error. [9]

Allison continues, "The first significant challenge to this belief did not arise until the seventeenth century."[10] He quotes a number of the church fathers to prove this is what the church has historically believed. For example, Clement of Rome wrote, "You have searched the Scriptures, which are true, which were given by the Holy Spirit; you know that nothing unrighteous or counterfeit is written in them."[11] Irenaeus wrote, "The Scriptures are indeed perfect."[12]

When the early church fathers spoke of the infallibility of Scripture, they were making two separate points. First, what Scripture affirms corresponds with reality. Tertullian wrote, "The statements of Holy Scripture will never be discordant with truth."[13] Augustine was even clearer: "I have learned to ascribe to those books which are of canonical rank and only to them, such reverence and honor that I firmly believe that no single error due to the author is found in any one of them."[14]

In addition to believing that what Scripture says corresponds to reality, they also believed it never contradicts itself. For example, Irenaeus wrote, "All Scripture, which has been given to us by God, shall be found by us perfectly consistent."[15] Justin Martyr, who was discipled by the apostle John, wrote "I am entirely convinced that no Scripture contradicts another."[16] Athanasius explained:

33

It is the opinion of some that the Scriptures do not agree or that God who gave them is false. But there is no disagreement at all. Far from it! Neither can the Father, who is truth, lie; 'for it is impossible that God should lie' [Heb. 6:18].[17]

This was also the view of the Reformers. In one example, Martin Luther writes, "Everyone, indeed knows that at times they [the fathers] have erred as men will; therefore, I am ready to trust them only when they prove their opinions from Scripture, which has never erred."[18] The Westminster Confession speaks of "the entire perfection" of Scripture and "the consent of all the parts."[19] Summarizing the consistent position of the church, Charles Hodge writes, "The Word of God, as contained in the Scriptures of the Old and New Testaments, is the only infallible rule of faith and practice."[20] Until the last several hundred years, church history spoke with almost one voice on the inerrancy of Scripture.

How did all the great minds of church history come to agree on this great truth? It's because this view is clearly biblical. Warfield asks:

How shall we account for the immediate adoption of so developed a doctrine of inspiration in the very infancy of the church and for the tenacious hold which the church has kept upon it through so many ages? ... This is the doctrine of inspiration which was held by the writers of the New Testament and by Jesus as reported in the

Gospels. It is this simple fact that has commended it to the church of all ages as the true doctrine.... This church-doctrine of inspiration was the Bible doctrine before it was the church-doctrine, and is the church-doctrine only because it is the Bible doctrine. [21]

The biblical argument is primarily twofold: 1) the claims Scripture makes for itself and 2) the statements of our Lord. To grasp what Scripture claims for itself, it is crucial to understand two passages in Deuteronomy. God first spoke through Moses, who wrote the first five books of our Old Testament, also known as the Law or the Pentateuch. No one doubted God spoke directly with Moses. Exodus 19 records that the two million Jews who came out of Egypt all gathered at the foot of Mount Sinai and watched Moses go up. Together they saw the dark cloud descend on the mountain, heard the thunder, and saw the lightning. They felt the earthquakes. They heard the heavenly trumpet grow louder and louder until it suddenly stopped. Then, out of the silence, they all heard God recite the Ten Commandments with His own voice! Moses stayed on the mountain with God and then came down to give them God's law. No one doubted Moses spoke for God.

But after Moses' death, how would God's people know who was an authentic messenger for God? Moses laid down two foundational criteria for identifying a true prophet. The first criterion is in Deuteronomy 13:1-5:

If a prophet or a dreamer of dreams arises among you and gives you a sign or a wonder, [someone claims to speak for God and is able to do the miraculous] *and the sign or the wonder comes true, concerning which he spoke to you, saying, 'Let us go after other gods (whom you have not known) and let us serve them,' you shall not listen to the words of that prophet or that dreamer of dreams; for the Lord your God is testing you to find out if you love the Lord your God with all your heart and with all your soul. You shall follow the Lord your God and fear Him; and you shall keep His commandments, listen to His voice, serve Him, and cling to Him. But that prophet or that dreamer of dreams shall be put to death, because he has counseled rebellion against the Lord your God who brought you from the land of Egypt and redeemed you from the house of slavery, to seduce you from the way in which the Lord your God commanded you to walk.*

The test of a prophet's genuineness is not primarily the power to work miracles. The crucial test is whether what he says agrees with previous revelation! If not, even if he works real miracles, he is not a true prophet.

Deuteronomy 18:20-22 adds a second criterion:

But the prophet who speaks a word presumptuously in My name which I have not commanded him to speak, or which he speaks in the name of other gods, that prophet shall die [notice, this addresses two different circumstances.

In one case a prophet claims to speak for the true God, and in the other a prophet speaks in the name of other gods]. *You may say in your heart, 'How will we know the word which the Lord has not spoken?' When a prophet speaks in the name of the Lord, if the thing does not come about or come true, that is the thing which the Lord has not spoken. The prophet has spoken it presumptuously; you shall not be afraid of him.*

The mark of a true prophet with a truly divine message was total truthfulness without a hint of error or falsehood. If his words distorted or contradicted *existing* revelation, he did not speak for God. And if his *new* revelation was wrong just once, he was not a true prophet, because God's words are always trustworthy.

Second Samuel 7:28 says, "O Lord God, You are God and Your words are truth." Psalm 12:6 says, "The words of the Lord are pure words; as silver tried in a furnace on the earth, refined seven times." Psalm 119:160 records, "The sum of Your word is truth, and every one of Your righteous ordinances is everlasting." All of it together is the truth without error, and every single ordinance is true.

In 2 Timothy 2:15, Paul told Timothy he needed to be a diligent workman, accurately handling the Scripture, which Paul called "the word of truth." In 2 Timothy 3:16, Paul directly stated that all Scripture is the product of the breath of God. If every word, letter, and stroke is breathed out by God, there can be no error, because God never deceives or lies. Numbers 23:19 says that "God is not a man, that He should lie." Hebrews 6:18 states that "it is impossible for God to lie." Scripture claims to be the breathed out, inerrant word of God.

The clear statements of our Lord make this same point. In the temptation, Satan tempted Jesus in three different ways. Jesus responded to each by quoting from the Old Testament. In Matthew 4:4, He quoted from Deuteronomy and affirmed what Moses wrote to be true: "Man shall not live on bread alone, but on every word that proceeds out of the mouth of God." Every word of our Bibles is the product of God's breath, and we are to rely on, depend on, and find our strength and sustenance in that Word more than even our necessary food.

In John 10:35, Jesus made the remarkable claim that "the Scripture cannot be broken." The word broken is the same word He used in Matthew 5:17—it means "to abolish." Scripture cannot be annulled, repealed, or abolished. Down to its individual words it will stand. In John 17:17, our Lord prays to the Father, "Your word is truth."

In Matthew 5:18, Jesus stated it this way: "Truly I say to you, until heaven and earth pass away, not the smallest letter or stroke shall pass from the Law until all is accomplished." The Greek word translated *accomplished* means "to happen or to come to pass." The entire universe could more easily disappear than for one statement of God to fail to come to pass. Jesus was affirming the utter trustworthiness, truthfulness, and certainty of the

Scripture. He was affirming its inerrancy down to the letters and the strokes.

Sadly, long ago many evangelicals surrendered inerrancy, and with it Genesis 1 and 2 and a literal six-day creation. And for years now, a battle has been raging in traditionally evangelical colleges and seminaries over whether Adam was a real, historical person. Where do such questions about the veracity of Scripture end? If Adam was not a real person, who can say Jesus was—or that He was raised from the dead? Jesus Himself had no such struggles regarding the truthfulness of God's Word. He believed God has given us a completely trustworthy Scripture in every detail. He believed its eternal authority, its verbal and plenary inspiration, and its complete inerrancy.

∵

SCRIPTURE'S CAREFUL PRESERVATION

∵

One final attribute of Scripture Jesus affirms here is its careful preservation. Although this is not directly stated, it is clearly implied. Jesus did not speak of the truthfulness of merely the ideas and thoughts in Scripture. He spoke of the letters and words in the *written* Scripture. When He affirmed that neither the smallest letter nor the smallest stroke would pass away, He implied God had preserved His Word up to that time in written form. By Jesus' day, of course, the original autographs had been lost. Instead, they relied, as we do, on copies that were ultimately made from those originals throughout generations. Yet Jesus consistently referred to those copies as "the Scripture." In fact, the Bible Jesus most frequently quoted was the Septuagint, a Greek translation made from those Hebrew copies. When He quoted from it and called it the Word of God, Jesus implied that the Scripture had been preserved down to His day.

Jesus often challenged the Jews about distorting the meaning of the Scripture, but He never once taught or implied that the text of Scripture they used had been corrupted. Instead, He quoted from both the Hebrew text and the Greek translation and called both "the Word of God."

Quoting the prophet Isaiah, Peter wrote, "All flesh is like grass, and all its glory like the flower of grass. The grass withers, and the flower falls off, but the word of the Lord endures forever" (1 Pet. 1:24-25). Then, Peter added, "And this is the word which was preached to you" (25). When Peter and the apostles preached from the Septuagint and the copies of the Hebrew manuscripts they possessed in the first century, they were preaching the enduring Word of God. Scripture has been remarkably preserved! When we consider the thousands of manuscripts of the Old and New Testaments that exist today, we too can have confidence that the Scripture has been preserved.[22]

Jesus believed and taught that those are the unchanging attributes of Scripture. As His followers, we must believe them as well. "A pupil is not above his teacher; but everyone, after he has been fully trained, will be like his teacher" (Luke 6:40). If Jesus is our teacher, we must embrace His view of Scripture.

In the next chapter, we discover a third response to Scripture that Jesus expects from His disciples.

CHAPTER THREE

ACCEPT JESUS' DIAGNOSIS WITH THE SCRIPTURE

"Whoever then annuls one of the least of these commandments, and teaches others to do the same, shall be called least in the kingdom of heaven; but whoever keeps and teaches them, he shall be called great in the kingdom of heaven. For I say to you that unless your righteousness surpasses that of the scribes and Pharisees, you will not enter the kingdom of heaven."

MATTHEW 5:19-20

∵

AMERICANS spend billions of dollars each year to maintain their physical health. We want to be physically healthy and to know that we are. Unfortunately, many of the tests that assure us we are healthy are also extremely intrusive and highly expensive. But doctors are working on a new kind of test—a simple diagnostic tool that will provide a window into our overall health using saliva. Researchers at M. D. Anderson have identified certain kinds of cancers from a simple mouth swab, and scientists at UT Austin believe they can predict future heart attacks by studying saliva.

But there is already a simple diagnostic tool that can discern our spiritual health—one simple test that provides a window into our spiritual condition. In verses 19-20, Jesus diagnoses the spiritual condition of three categories of people. And His sole diagnostic tool is their relationship to the Word of God. They all claim to have a relationship with the true God, but in each case their response to Scripture reveals their true spiritual condition.

⁛

THE DISHONORABLE DISCIPLE

⁛

"Whoever then annuls one of the least of these commandments, and teaches others to do the same, shall be called least in the kingdom of heaven" (19a). Jesus confirms that this person is in His spiritual kingdom now and will be in His future kingdom when He reigns on this earth. So, this is a true Christian.

But notice how he treats Scripture. He feels free to *annul* its lesser commandments.[1] The Greek word annul was used literally of untying an animal. Figuratively, it means to loose oneself from a document and its commands so that it no longer has authority over you. This Christian minimizes or downplays portions of Scripture. Christ's point is that we cannot disregard the least significant portion of Scripture without having been authorized to do so either by Him or by His apostles.[2] Every command, even the insignificant, is important and must be kept.

The dishonorable disciple not only disregards the commandment himself but teaches others to do the same as well. He uses his influence to convince others to downplay the commands of Scripture in their own lives—by his example, his attitude, his conversation, and perhaps even his teaching.

He "shall be called [*that's a divine passive—in context, Christ Himself will call him*] least in the kingdom of heaven" (19). The word least means inferior in status or in quality. Jesus said He will call the true Christian who downplays or minimizes any portion of Scripture least in His future kingdom. John MacArthur writes:

> *Jesus declares that He will hold those in lowest esteem who hold His Word in lowest esteem.... Greatness is not determined by gifts, success, popularity, reputation, or size of ministry—but by a believer's view of Scripture as revealed in his life and teaching.*[3]

∵

THE HONORABLE DISCIPLE

∵

"But whoever keeps and teaches them, he shall be called great in the kingdom of heaven" (19b). This person, too, will be in the kingdom, but his response to Scripture is different than the first. The Greek word translated *keeps* is the normal word for *do*. He responds to Scripture in obedience. He doesn't set aside even the least Old Testament command. Instead, he commits himself to obeying the whole Scripture, even those commands that seem insignificant.

The honorable disciple not only endeavors to personally obey all Scripture, but he also uses his influence to magnify and exalt the Scripture in the minds of others. He honors and exalts it in his life and teaching. "He shall be called great in the kingdom of heaven." Christ will honor the believer who exalts and honors the Scripture. William Hendriksen writes, "Although all is of grace and nothing whatever is *earned* by the citizen of the kingdom, yet his rank or position in that kingdom will depend on and be commensurate with his respect for God's holy law."[4] The point is this: in the future Jesus will honor those who honor His Word now.

∵
THE FALSE DISCIPLE
∵

"For I say to you that unless your righteousness surpasses that of the scribes and Pharisees, you will not enter the kingdom of heaven" (20). Some who attach themselves to Jesus do not belong to His spiritual kingdom now and will not enter His physical kingdom in the future. For all who think they are Christians, it comes down to this: does our righteousness surpass the righteousness of the scribes and Pharisees? Of course, that raises the crucial question: how was their righteousness deficient?

Their righteousness was fatally flawed in two ways. First, it was self-righteousness. It was rotten at its foundation. They missed the whole point of the Old Testament Scriptures. The point of the Law was to show us our sin and utter lack of personal righteousness and drive us to the Messiah as our only hope of real righteousness (Gal. 3:19-24). The scribes and the Pharisees missed that message entirely. They thought they simply needed to keep God's law to achieve a right standing before Him (Luke 16:14-15; 18:11-12; Rom. 10:3).

But in Matthew 5 Jesus is chiefly referring to a second way their righteousness was flawed. Not only was it self-righteousness, but it was also imperfect—in several crucial ways. It was external, and not internal (Matt. 23:25-26; Mark 7:6). It was self-centered and not for God's glory (Matt. 23:5). It was incomplete and not radical. They obeyed the easier, less important commands but failed to obey the most important ones (Matt. 23:23). In Matthew 5, Jesus gave six examples of how their distorted interpretation of Scripture changed what God intended into something else entirely. What God wants is radical obedience: "Therefore you are to be perfect, as your heavenly Father is perfect" (5:48).

CONCLUSION

∴

AS Jesus' disciples, like our Lord, we must embrace and champion a high view of Scripture. And our behavior will always betray the reality of that belief. If we believe about the Scripture what our Lord did, we will treat the Scripture as He did:

1) He taught the Scripture as the focus of His ministry and demanded that people place themselves under its authority. The thrust of Jesus' ministry was not primarily the miracles He performed but the teaching of the Word of God. When the crowds grew because of His miracles and His disciples pled with Him to stay, Jesus responded, "Let us go somewhere else to the towns nearby, so that I may preach there also; for that is what I came for." (Mark 1:38). A biblical pastor and a biblical church will have the same priorities.

2) He read the Scripture and expected others to read it. "Beginning with Moses and with all the prophets, He explained to them the things concerning Himself in all the Scriptures" (Luke 24:27). He read, knew, and explained all the Scriptures. In Mark 12:10, He said to the Jews, "Have you not even read the Scripture?" If we share Jesus' high view of Scripture, we will read it.

3) He memorized Scripture and used it against temptation. When Satan tempted Him in the wilderness, three times Jesus quoted Deuteronomy and said, "It is written." That is how we must respond to temptation as well. We must not only memorize it but also have a profound grasp of its meaning, so that it is not merely a mantra.

4) He studied the Scripture. When He was only 12 years old, His parents accidentally left Him in Jerusalem. Three days later they found Him in the temple "in the midst of the teachers, both listening to them and asking them questions" (Luke 2:46). As a human being, He was seeking to grow in His knowledge of the Scripture. We must as well.

5) He obeyed Scripture and expects us to as well. He said, "I have kept My Father's commandments and abide in His love" (John 15:10). He explained the implication for His disciples: "If you keep My commandments, you will abide in My love" (John 15:10). In Luke 8, it was reported to Jesus that His mother and brothers were outside waiting for Him. He pointed to the followers around Him and said, "My mother and My brothers are these who hear the word of God and do it" (Luke 8:21). We are related to Jesus if we hear God's Word and do it.

∵

VOICES FROM THE PAST

∵

W HAT follows are select quotes from church history that show a consistently high view of Scripture throughout the centuries. In particular, these voices from church history magnify the divine nature and character of the Word of God.

∵

CLEMENT OF ROME (D. CA. 95)

You have studied the Holy Scriptures, which are true and inspired by the Holy Spirit. You know that nothing contrary to justice or truth has been written in them.[1]

IRENAEUS OF LYONS (CA. 130-202)

The Scriptures are indeed perfect since they were spoken by the Word of God and His Spirit.[2]

TERTULLIAN (CA. 155-200)

The statements of Holy Scripture will never be discordant with truth.[3]

ATHANASIUS (CA. 296-373)

Now it is the opinion of some, that the Scriptures do not agree together, or that God, Who gave the commandment, is false. But there is no disagreement whatever, far from it, neither can the Father, Who is truth, lie.[4]

∵

These [books] are the fountains of salvation, so that those who are thirsty may be satisfied by the living words they contain. In these alone the teaching godliness is proclaimed. Let no one add to these; let nothing be taken away from them.[5]

JOHN CHRYSOSTOM (CA. 347-407)

For the Scripture by no means speaks falsely.[6]

AUGUSTINE OF HIPPO (354-430)

I have learned to ascribe to those books of canonical rank, and only to them, such reverence and honor, that I firmly believe that no single error, due to the author, is found in any one of them.[7]

∵

I think it is extremely dangerous to admit that anything in the Sacred Book should be a lie.... If we once admit in that supreme authority even one polite lie, there will be nothing left of those books, because, whenever anyone finds something difficult to practice or hard to believe, he will follow his most dangerous precedent and explain it as the idea or practice of a lying author.[8]

∵

For, I admit to your charity that it is from those books alone of the Scriptures, which are now called canonical, that I have learned to pay them such honor and respect as to believe most firmly that not one of their authors has erred in writing anything at all. If I do find anything in those books which seems contrary to truth, I decide that either the text is corrupt, or the translator did not follow what was really said, or that I failed to understand it.[9]

⁙

Whoever understands Scripture in a way that the writer did not intend goes astray, but not because there is anything wrong in Scripture.[10]

⁙

The Mediator spoke in former times through the prophets and later through his own mouth, and after that through the apsotles, telling man all that he decided was enough for man [to know]. He also instituted the Scripture that we call canonical. These are the writings of outstanding authority in which we put our trust concerning those things that need to know for our own good, but cannot discover by ourselves.[11]

ANSELM OF CANTERBURY (1033-1109)

I am sure that, if I say anything which is undoubtedly contradictory to Holy Scripture, it is wrong; and, if I become aware of such a contradiction, I do not wish to hold to that opinion.[12]

HULDRYCH ZWINGLI (1484-1531)

So then we have come to the point where, from the fact that we are the image of God, we may see that there is nothing which can give greater joy or assurance or comfort to the soul than the Word of its creator and maker. We can now apply ourselves to understand the clarity and infallibility of the Word of God.[13]

PHILIP MELANCHTHON (1497-1560)

We should understand that it is a great blessing of God that He has given to His church a certain Book, and He preserves it for us and gathers His church around it. Finally, the church is the people who embrace this Book, hear, learn, and retain as their own its teachings in their worship life and in the governing of their morals.[14]

MARTIN LUTHER (1483-1546)

Everyone indeed knows that, at times, they (church fathers) have erred as men will. Therefore, I am ready to trust them only when they prove their opinions from Scripture which has never erred.[15]

∵

Where Holy Scripture is the ground of faith we are not to deviate from the words as they stand nor from the order in which they stand, unless an express article of faith compels a different interpretation or order. For else, what would happen to the Bible?[16]

HEINRICH BULLINGER (1504-1575)

Let us therefore in all things believe the word of God delivered to us by the scriptures. Let us think that the Lord himself, which is the very living and eternal God, doth speak to us by the scriptures. Let us for evermore praise the name and goodness of him, who hath vouchedsafed so faithfully, fully, and plainly to open to us, miserable mortal men, all the means how to live well and holily.[17]

JOHN CALVIN (1509-1564)

We owe to the Scripture the same reverence as we owe God, since it has its only source in Him and has nothing of human origin mixed with it.[18]

JOHN OWEN (1616-1683)

It follows that our faith, whereby we believe any divine, supernatural truth, is resolved into the Scripture, as the only means of divine revelation, affecting our minds and consciences with the authority and truth of God; or, the Scripture, as the only immediate, divine, infallible revelation of the mind and will of God, is the first immediate formal object of our faith, the sole reason why and ground whereon we do believe the things that are revealed with faith divine, supernatural, and infallible.[19]

JONATHAN EDWARDS (1703-1758)

Hence we may learn that all the Scripture says to us is certainly true.... Consider how much it is worth the while to go often to your Bible to hear the great God Himself speak to you. There you may hear Christ speak. How much better must we think this is than the word of men.... Here all is true; nothing false.[20]

JOHN BROWN (1722-1787)

The revelations contained in our Bibles are divinely inspired, proceeding from an infinitely wise, holy, just, true, and infallible God.[21]

CHARLES HODGE (1797-1878)

The infallibility and divine authority of the Scriptures are due to the fact they are the word of God; and they are the word of God because they were given by the inspiration of the Holy Ghost.[22]

J. C. RYLE (1816-1900)

The Bible is utterly unlike all other books that were ever written because its writers were specially inspired, or enabled by God, for the work which they did. I say that the Book comes to us with a claim which no other book possesses. It is stamped with divine authority. In this respect it stands entirely alone. Sermons, and tracts, and theological writings of all kinds, may be sound and edifying but they are only the handiwork of uninspired man. The Bible alone is the Book of God.[23]

WILLIAM G. T. SHEDD (1820-1894)

The infallibility and authority which distinguish the Scriptures from all other books, are due to the Divine authorship. But God employed various modes in this authorship (Heb. 1:1–2).... Here, the prophets of the Old Testament, and Christ, the subject of the revelation, are mentioned as the media through whom the Divine Mind was communicated. To these, must be added the apostles of the New Testament.[24]

A. A. HODGE (1823-1886)

That sacred writings were so influenced by the Holy Spirit that their writings are as a whole and in every part God's word to us—an authoritative revelation to us from God, endorsed by him, and sent to us as a rule of faith and practice, the original autographs of which are absolutely infallible when interpreted in the sense intended, and hence are clothed with absolute divine authority.[25]

CHARLES HADDON SPURGEON (1834-1892)

[Jesus] knew by His omniscience what was the most instructive way of teaching, and by turning at once to Moses and the prophets, He showed us that the surest road to wisdom is not speculation, reasoning, or reading human books, but meditation upon the Word of God. The readiest way to be spiritually rich in heavenly knowledge is to dig in the mine of diamonds, to gather pearls from this heavenly sea. When Jesus Himself sought to enrich others, He wrought in the quarry of Holy Scripture.[26]

B. B. WARFIELD (1851-1921)

That the Scriptures are throughout a Divine book, created by the Divine energy and speaking in their every part with Divine authority directly to the heart of the readers, is the fundamental fact concerning them which is witnessed by Christ and the sacred writers to whom we own the New Testament.... The whole of Scripture in all its parts and in all its elements, down to the least minutiae, in form of expression as well as in substance of teaching, is from God.[27]

GEERHARDUS VOS (1862-1949)

The underlying supposition of all arguing from Scripture as, in common with others, our Lord practiced it, consists in this, that the Word of God has received from Him the quality of unbreakableness; not to believe involves an attempt to break something that God has declared sure.[28]

A. W. PINK (1886-1952)

The written Word is (not "contains") unadulterated truth, because its Author cannot lie. In it there is no error. Because the Word is God's truth it is of final authority. By it everything is to be tested. By it our thoughts are to be formed and our conduct is to be regulated.... If then the Word is truth what a high value we should put upon it.... How dearly we should prize it.[29]

MARTYN LLOYD-JONES (1899-1981)

Inspired really means "God-breathed." We mean that God breathed these messages into men and through them, and these Scriptures are the result of that divine action. We believe that they were produced by the creative breath of the Almighty God. Put in a simpler form, we mean that everything we have here has been given by God to man.... It is not merely that the thoughts are inspired, not merely the ideas, but the actual record, down to the particular words. It is not merely that the statements are correct, but that every word is divinely inspired.[30]

R. C. SPROUL (1939-2017)

If the Lord God Almighty opens His mouth, there is no room for debate and no excuse for unbelief. [Holy Scripture] is the Word of God, and everyone is duty-bound to submit to its authority.[31]

NOTES

⁚

INTRODUCTION

1.   Organization of the Sermon on the Mount:

I. The Citizens of the Kingdom (5:3-16)

A. Their Character (3-12)

B. Their Influence (13-16)

II. The Righteousness of the Kingdom (5:17—7:12)

A. A Right Relationship to Scripture (5:17-48)

a. Explained (17-20)

b. Illustrated (21-47)

c. Summarized (48)

B. A Right Relationship to God (6:1-34)

a. Unhypocritical Spirituality (1-18)

b. Undivided Devotion (19-24)

c. Unwavering Trust (25-34)

C. A Right Relationship to Others (7:1-12)

III. The Dangers of the Kingdom (7:13-27)

A. Beware of the Wrong Entrance (13-14)

B. Beware of the False Teachers (15-20)

C. Beware of a False Profession (21-27)

CHAPTER 1:
UNDERSTAND JESUS' OWN RELATIONSHIP TO SCRIPTURE

1. Believers in the first century used the Septuagint, a Greek translation of the Hebrew Scripture that included the Apocrypha. But the books of the Apocrypha were never considered to be part of the Hebrew canon. Josephus, the Jewish commander who was captured and later became a friend of Rome, wrote a history of the Jewish nation. In the second half of the first century, Josephus, who used the Septuagint, writes [Contra Apion, 1:8], "We have not tens of thousands of books, discordant and conflicting, but only twenty-two [the books of our Old Testament not counting the Apocrypha] containing the record of all time which had been justly believed to be divine." Then, he adds regarding the Apocrypha: "From Artaxerxes, [around the time of Ezra] to our own times, a complete history has been written but has not been deemed worthy of equal credit with the earlier records because of the failure of the exact succession of the prophets." Since the books of the Apocrypha were not written by men who were clearly prophets of God, they were not accepted at the same level as the twenty-two books of the Hebrew canon. Josephus adds, "No words of God had been added to the Scripture since 400 BC with the last OT author." That is why our Lord and His apostles quote the canonical OT books and introduce their quotes with "Thus it is written" or a similar expression almost 295 times. But not one time do they quote the Apocrypha as authoritative, even though it was attached to their Bible.

CHAPTER 2:

EMBRACE JESUS' VIEW OF SCRIPTURE

1. Benjamin Breckinridge Warfield, Samuel G. Craig, and Cornelius Van Til, *The Inspiration and Authority of the Bible* (Philadelphia: Presbyterian and Reformed, 1948), 106.

2. Ibid., 119.

3. Gregg R. Allison, *Historical Theology* (Grand Rapids: Zondervan, 2011), 62.

4. Ibid., 61-62.

5. R. Laird Harris, *Inspiration and Canonicity of the Scriptures* (Greenville, SC: A Press, 1995), 35.

6. John Wenham, *"Christ's View of Scripture,"* *Inerrancy*, ed. Norman Geisler (Grand Rapids: Zondervan, 1980), 6.

7. Allison, *Historical Theology*, 102.

8. Paul Feinberg, *"The Meaning of Inerrancy,"* *Inerrancy*, ed. Norman Geisler (Grand Rapids: Zondervan, 1982), 294.

9. Allison, *Historical Theology*, 99.

10. Ibid.

11. Ibid., 100.

12. Ibid.

13. Ibid.

14. Carl F. H. Henry, *God, Revelation, and Authority* (Waco, Texas: Word Books, 1983), 370-72.

15. Allison, *Historical Theology*, 100.

16. Ibid.

17. Ibid., 101.

18. Jonathan Moorehead, *"Inerrancy & Church History: Is Inerrancy a Modern Invention?,"* The Master's Seminary Journal 27/1 (Spring 2016), 82.

19. *The Westminster Confession of Faith* (Carlisle, PA: Banner of Truth, 2012), 20.

20. Charles Hodge, *Systematic Theology, Vol. 1, Theology* (Grand Rapids: Baker, 1975), 151.

21. Warfield, *The Inspiration and Authority of the Bible*, 114.

22. There are more extant manuscripts of the Bible than any other ancient document: 3000 of the OT and 25,000 of the NT. The second largest number of manuscripts of an ancient document is Homer's *Iliad* with only 1800. The 25,000 NT manuscripts include a) more than 5700 Greek manuscripts of the NT that date from 125 A.D. to about 1200 A.D. (cf. that with less than 20 manuscripts for most of the classical Greek and Roman works); b) more than 19,000 early translations, like Latin, Syriac, and Coptic. In addition, there are more than 1 million quotations of Scripture in the writings of the early church fathers. Scholars estimate that if all manuscripts of the NT had been lost, from the early church fathers' quotations alone we could reconstruct almost the entire NT (Bruce Metzger & Bart Ehrman, *The Text of the New Testament*), except for about 11 verses, mostly from 2nd and 3rd John (Norman Geisler, *When Skeptics Ask*). With other ancient documents, there is a large gap of time between when the events occurred and the date of the extant manuscripts. For example, our earliest manuscripts of the classic Greek and Roman works were copied 700 to 1400 years after the originals were written. But there are complete manuscripts of the NT copied only 150 years after the events they describe. And the Rylands papyrus, which records a small portion of John's gospel, dates to 25 years after it was written. By every standard used with ancient documents, the evidence for the reliability of the Bible is overwhelming.

CHAPTER 3:
ACCEPT JESUS' DIAGNOSIS WITH THE SCRIPTURE

1. Jesus contrasts some of the greater and lesser commands of Scripture in Matthew 23:23.

2. For example, Christ authorizes the eating of unclean animals when He declares all foods clean (Mark 7:19; cf. 1 Tim. 4:3-5). Paul, writing under the inspiration of the Spirit, declares that NT believers are no longer required to keep the weekly sabbaths, new moon celebrations, or annual Jewish festivals required under OT law (Col. 2:16-17). Hebrews affirms that the entire sacrificial system was fulfilled in Christ and is no longer binding on New Covenant Christians.

3. John MacArthur, *The MacArthur New Testament Commentary: Matthew, Vol. 1* (Chicago: Moody, 1985), 270, 272.

4. William Hendriksen, *New Testament Commentary: Exposition of the Gospel According to Matthew* (Grand Rapids: Baker, 2007), 292.

APPENDIX:
VOICES FROM THE PAST

1. Clement, *Letter to the Corinthians*, 45 in *MG* 1, 300; FC I, 42. Cited in John R. Willis, *The Teachings of the Church Fathers* (New York, NY: Herder and Herder, 1966), 107.

2. Irenaeus, *Against Heresies*, 2.28.2 in MG 7, 804; ANF I, 399. Cited in Ibid., 108.

3. Tertullian, *A Treatise on the Soul*, 21 in *ANF*, 3:202.

4. Athanasius, *Letter 19:3* in *ANF*, 546. Cited in Jonathan Moorehead, *"Inerrancy and Church History: Is Inerrancy a Modern Invention?,"* 78.

5. Athanasius of Alexandria., *Epsitula festalis 39* (AD 367). See Metzger *Canon of the New Testament*, 211-212. Cited in Gerald Bray, *God Has Spoken: A*

History of Christian Theology (Wheaton, IL: Crossway, 2014), 743.

6.   John Chrystostom, *"Concerning the Statues,"* 2.22 in *NPNF*, edited by Philip Schaff (Peabody: Hendrickson Publishers, 1999), 9:352. Cited in Moorehead, *"Inerrancy and Church History: Is Inerrancy a Modern Invention?,"* 78.

7.   Augustine, *Epistulae*, 82.3, in *CSEL* 33:354. Cited in Matthew Barrett, *Reformation Theology: A Systematic Summary* (Wheaton, IL: Crossway, 2017), 148.

8.   Augustine, Letter 28 in *ML* 33, 112; *FC* XII 95-96. Cited in Willis, *The Teachings of the Church Fathers*, 114.

9.   Augustine, Letter 82 in *ML* 33 277; *FC* XII, 392. Cited in Ibid., 114.

10. Augustine of Hippo., *De doctrina Christiana* 1.36 (41). Cited in Bray, *God Has Spoken: A History of Christian Theology*, 756.

11. Augustine of Hippo, *De civitate De*i 11.3. Cited in Ibid., 757.

12. Anselm, *Why God Became Man*, in *Anselm of Canterbury: The Major Works* (Oxford: Oxford University Press, 2008), 298. Cited in Moorehead, *"Inerrancy and Church History: Is Inerrancy a Modern Invention?,"* 81.

13. Huldrych Zwingli, *Von der gewüsse oder kraft des worts gottes* (1522), in ZSW 1:352-53; English translation in *Swingli and Bullinger: Selected Translations with Intoductions and Notes*, ed G. W. Bromiley, LCC 24 (Philadelphia: Westminster, 1953), 68. Cited in Barrett, *Reformation Theology: A Systematic Summary*, 165.

14. Philipp Melanchthon, *Loci Communes* (1543), *CR* 21:801; Melanchthon, *Loci Communes* 1543, trans. J. A. O. Preus (St. Louis, MO: Concordia, 1992), 117. Cited in Ibid., 163.

15. Martin Luther, *Works of Martin Luther* (St. Louis, MO: Concordia Publishing House, 1968), 32.11.

16. Martin Luther, *Wider die himmlischen Propheten von den Bildern und Sakrament* (1525), WA 18:147.23-26; LW 40:157. Cited in Barrett, *Reformation Theology: A Systematic Summary*, 155.

17. Heinrich Bullinger, *Sermonum Decades quinque, de potissimis Christianae religionis capitibus* (Zurich: Froschoveri, 1557), 5; *The Decades of Henry Bullinger, Minister of the Church of Zurich*, trans. H. I., ed. Thomas Harding, Parker Society for the Publication of the Words of the Fathers and Early Writers of the Reformed English Church 7-10 (1587; repr., Cambridge: Cambridge University Press, 1849), 56-57. Cited in Ibid., 170.

18. John Calvin, *Calvin's Commentaries: The Second Epistle of Paul the Apostle to the Corinthians and the Epistles to Timothy, Titus and Philemon*, ed. D. W. and T. F. Torrance (Edinburgh: St. Andrew Press, 1964), 330 (2 Tim. 3:16).

19. John Owen, *The Works of John Owen*, Vol. 4, *The Work of the Spirit* (Carlisle, PA: Banner of Truth, 1967), 19.

20. Jonathan Edwards, *"2 Tim. iii.16–'All scripture is given by inspiration of God'" in Selections from the Unpublished Writings of Jonathan Edwards of America*, edited by Rev. Alexander Grosart (Ligonier, PA: Soli Deo Gloria Publications, 1992), 194-95. Cited in Moorehead, *"Inerrancy and Church History: Is Inerrancy a Modern Invention?,"* 85.

21. John Brown, *The Systematic Theology of John Brown of Haddington* (Grand Rapids: Reformation Heritage, 2002), 69.

22. Charles Hodge, *Systematic Theology*, Vol. 1, *Theology* (New York, NY: Charles Scribner's Sons, 1898), 153.

23. J. C. Ryle, *Is All Scripture Inspired?* (Carlisle, PA: Banner of Truth, 2003), 5.

24. William G. T. Shedd, *Dogmatic Theology*, Vol 1 (Charles Scribner's Sons, 1891), 109.

25. A. A. Hodge, *Outlines of Theology* (Carlisle, PA: Banner of Truth, 1972), 66.

26. Charles H. Spurgeon, *Morning and Evening: Daily Readings* (Mclean, VA: MacDonald Publishing, 1991), 37.

27. Benjamin B. Warfield, *The Works of Benjamin B. Warfied*, Vol. 1, *Revelation and Inspiration* (Grand Rapids; Baker, 2003), 96.

28. Geerhardus Vos, *Biblical Theology: Old and New Testaments* (Carlisle, PA: Banner of Truth, 1975), 360.

29. A. W. Pink, *Exposition of the Gospel of John*, Vol. 3 (Grand Rapids: Zondervan, 1975), 135.

30. Martyn Lloyd-Jones, *Great Doctrines of the Bible* (Carlisle, PA: Banner of Truth, 2003), 24.

31. R. C. Sproul, *Truths We Confess: A Systematic Exposition of the Westminter Confession of Faith*, rev.ed. (Sanford, FL: Reformation Trust, 2019), 13.

SCRIPTURE INDEX

ABOUT THE AUTHOR

∵

Tom PENNINGTON has served as Pastor-Teacher at Countryside Bible Church in Southlake, Texas since 2003. Prior to arriving in Texas, Tom served in various roles at Grace Community Church in Sun Valley, California for 16 years. His ministry at Grace included being an elder, Senior Associate Pastor, and the personal assistant to John MacArthur. Tom was also an adjunct faculty member of The Master's Seminary and Managing Director of Grace to You.

Tom is a graduate of Bob Jones University and holds an honorary Doctor of Divinity (D.D.) from The Master's University.

In addition to his role at Countryside, Tom travels internationally to train pastors in expository preaching.

He serves as Dean of the Dallas Distance Location at The Master's Seminary, teaches various seminary courses, and is actively involved internationally in training pastors in expository preaching.

Tom's preaching and teaching ministry at Countryside provides the source material for the content on The Word Unleashed.

ALSO AVAILABLE FROM TOM PENNINGTON

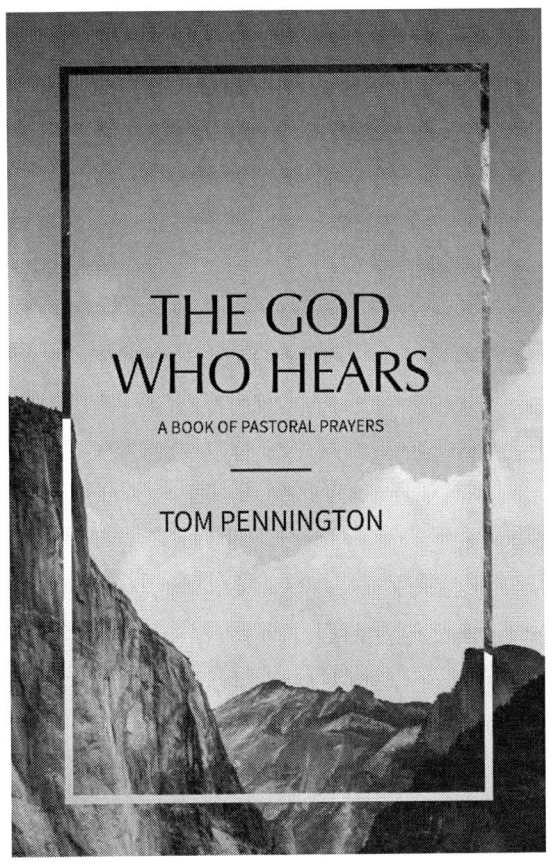

THE GOD
WHO HEARS
A BOOK OF PASTORAL PRAYERS

TOM PENNINGTON

www.**TheWordUnleashed**.org
www.**CountrysideBible**.org

PERSONAL NOTES

⁘

....
....
....
....
....
....
....
....
....
....
....
....
....
....
....
....
....
....
....
....
....
....